The outlines of the old hill fort on Cleeve Hill

THE COTSWOLD WAY

The Cotswold Way National Trail runs between charming Chipping Camden in Gloucestershire and the Roman spa town of Bath. The 102-mile route explores the Cotswolds Area of Outstanding Natural Beauty. Typically taking up to a fortnight to walk, the Cotswold Way would make an ideal introduction to long-distance walking.

Contents and using this guide

This booklet of Ordnance Survey 1:25,000 Explorer® maps has been designed for convenient use on the trail and includes:

- a key to map pages (page 2) showing where to find the maps for each stage.
- the full and up-to-date line of the National Trail, designed for use northbound or southbound.
- an extract from OS Explorer map legend (pages 44–46).

The companion guidebook – *The Cotswold Way* – describes the full route in both directions with lots of other practical and historical information.

© Cicerone Press 2024
ISBN: 978 1 78631 211 2
Second edition 2024
First edition 2016

Photos © Jonathan and Lesley Williams
© Crown copyright and database rights 2024 OS AC0000810376

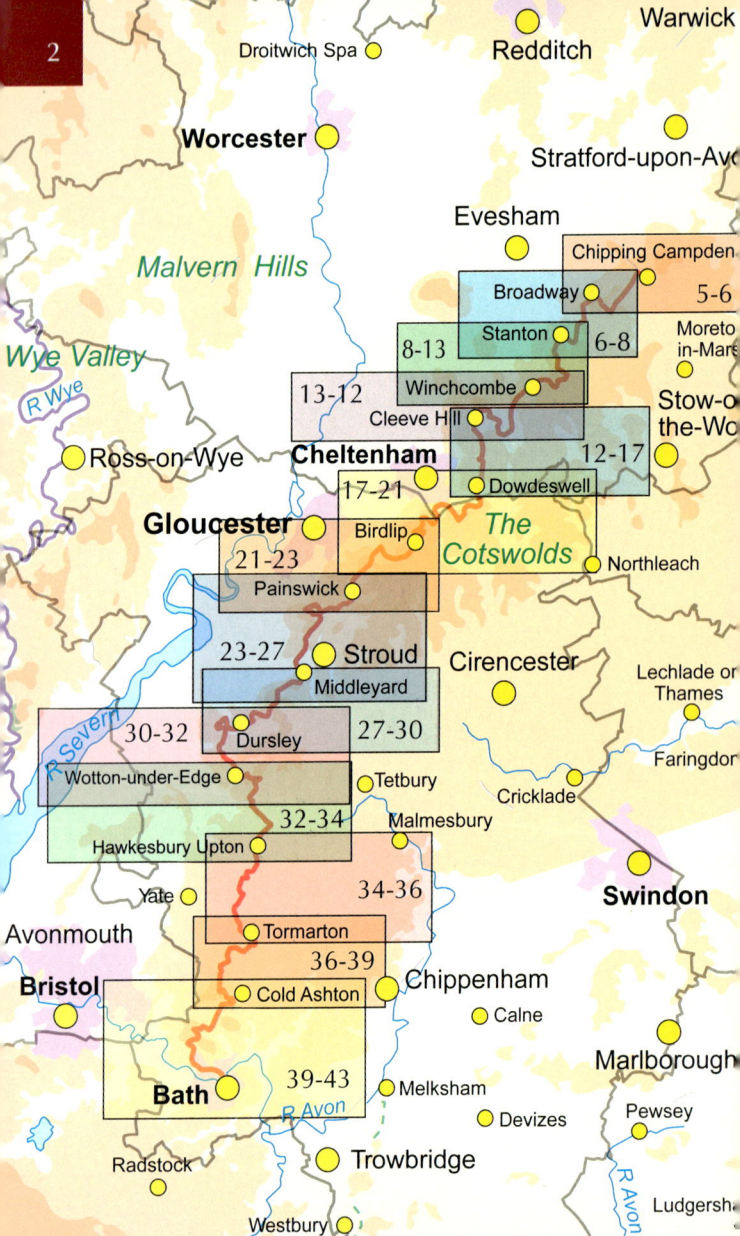

THE COTSWOLD WAY

Stage 1	Chipping Campden to Broadway	5
Stage 2	Broadway to Stanton	6
Stage 3	Stanton to Winchcombe	8
Stage 4	Winchcombe to Cleeve Hill	13
Stage 5	Cleeve Hill to Dowdeswell	12
Stage 6	Dowdeswell to Birdlip	17
Stage 7	Birdlip to Painswick	21
Stage 9	Painswick to Middleyard (King's Stanley)	23
Stage 9	Middleyard (King's Stanley) to Dursley	27
Stage 10	Dursley to Wotton-under-Edge	30
Stage 11	Wotton-under-Edge to Hawkesbury Upton	32
Stage 12	Hawkesbury Upton to Tormarton	34
Stage 13	Tormarton to Cold Ashton	36
Stage 14	Cold Ashton to Bath	39

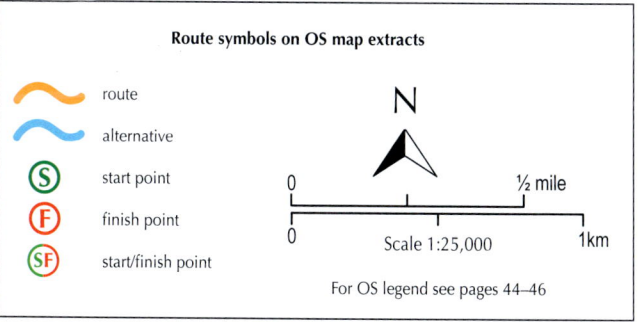

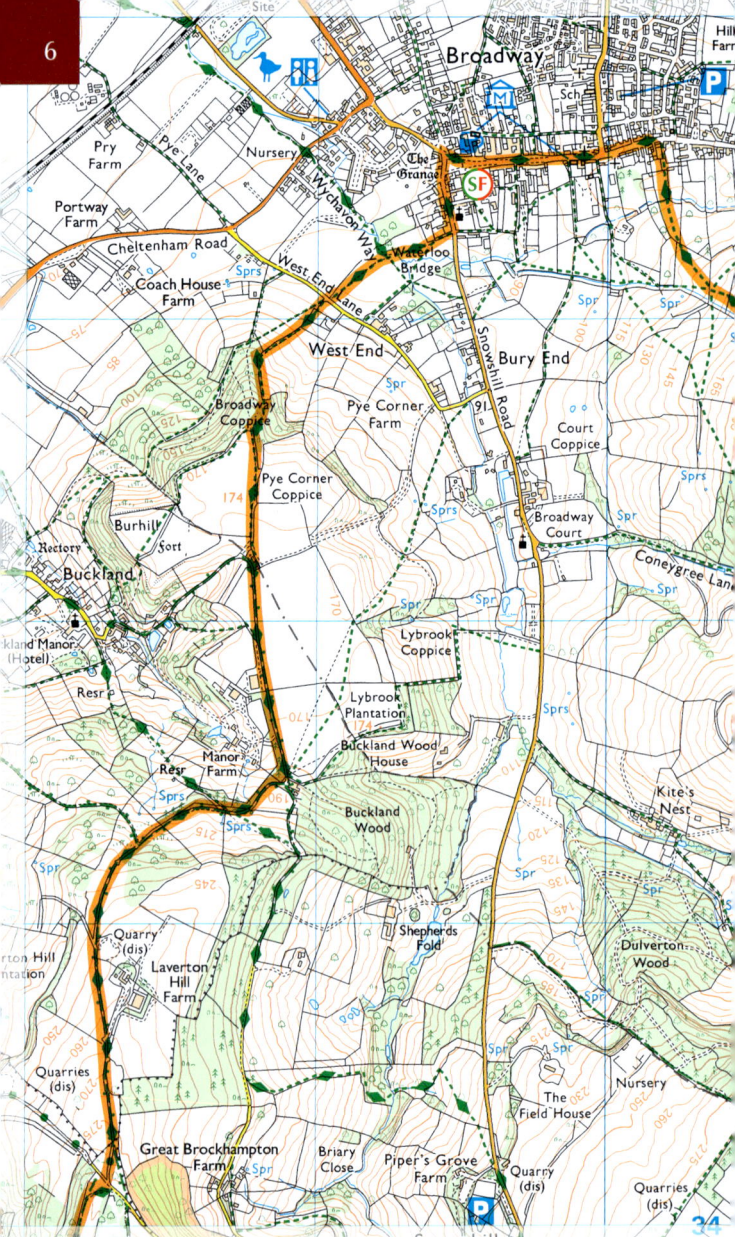

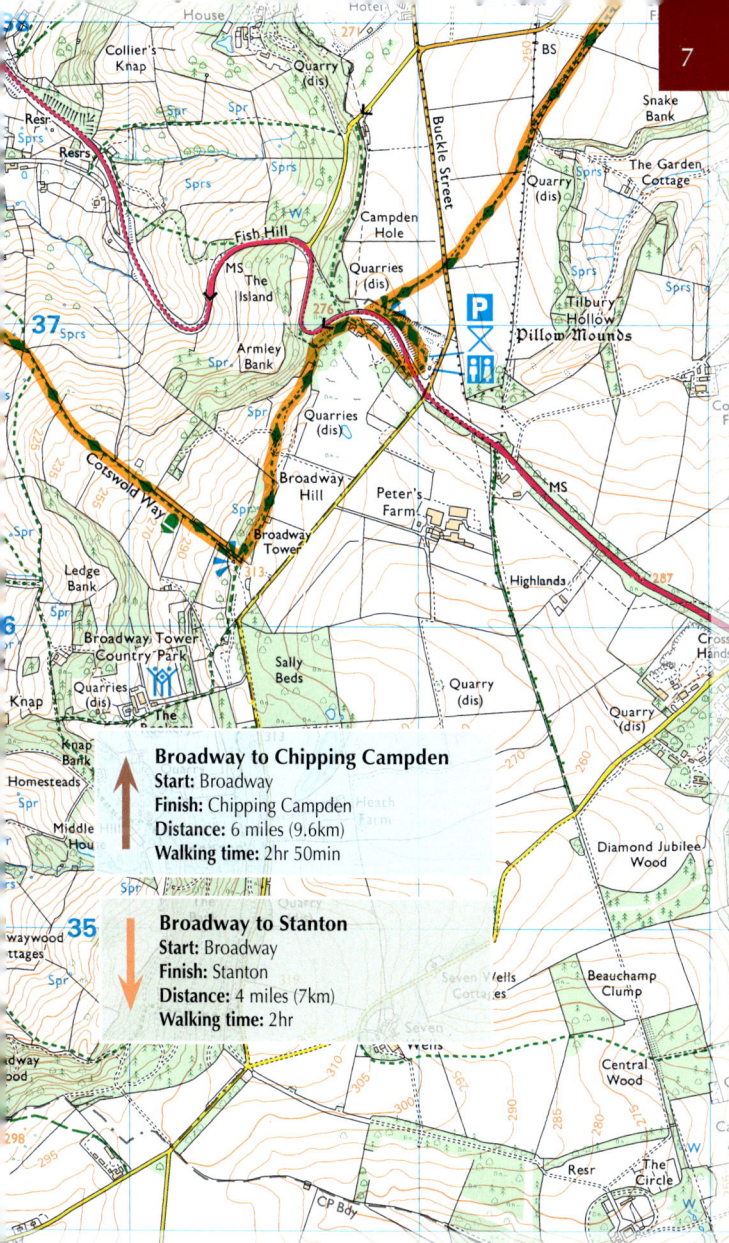

Stanton to Winchcombe
Start: Stanton
Finish: Winchcombe
Distance: 7¾ miles (12.3km)
Walking time: 3hr 15min

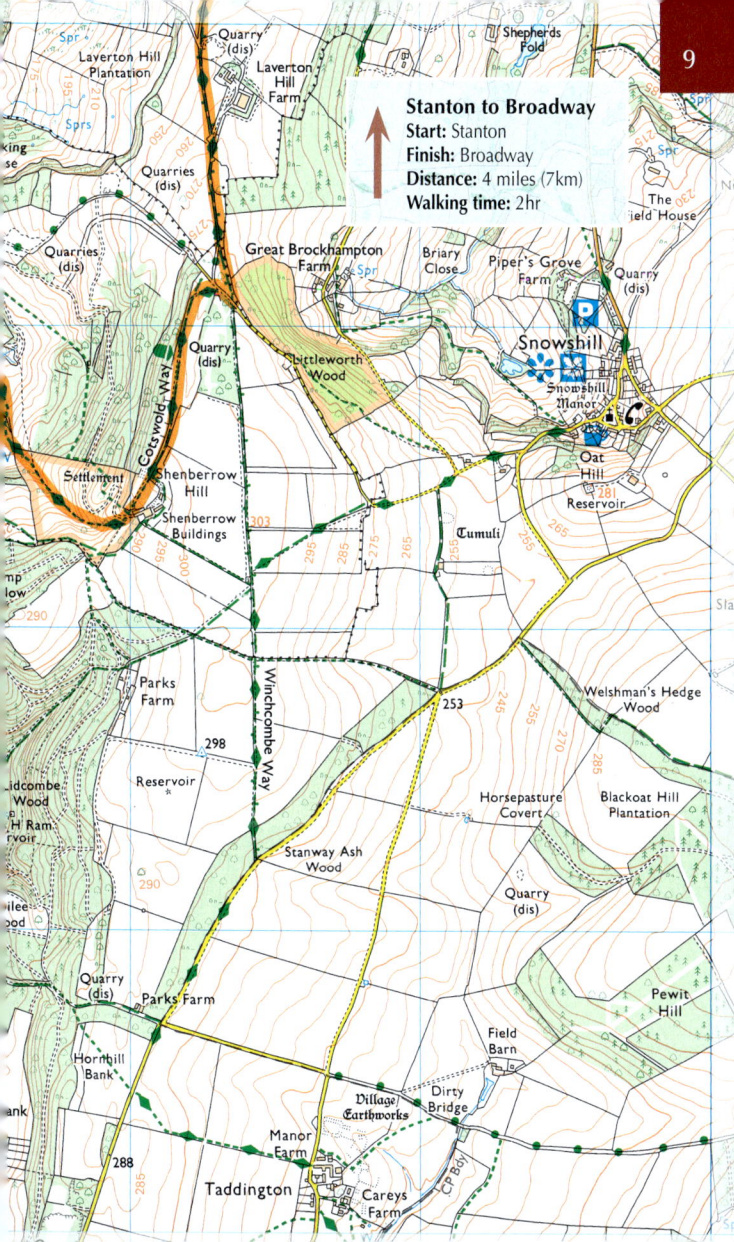

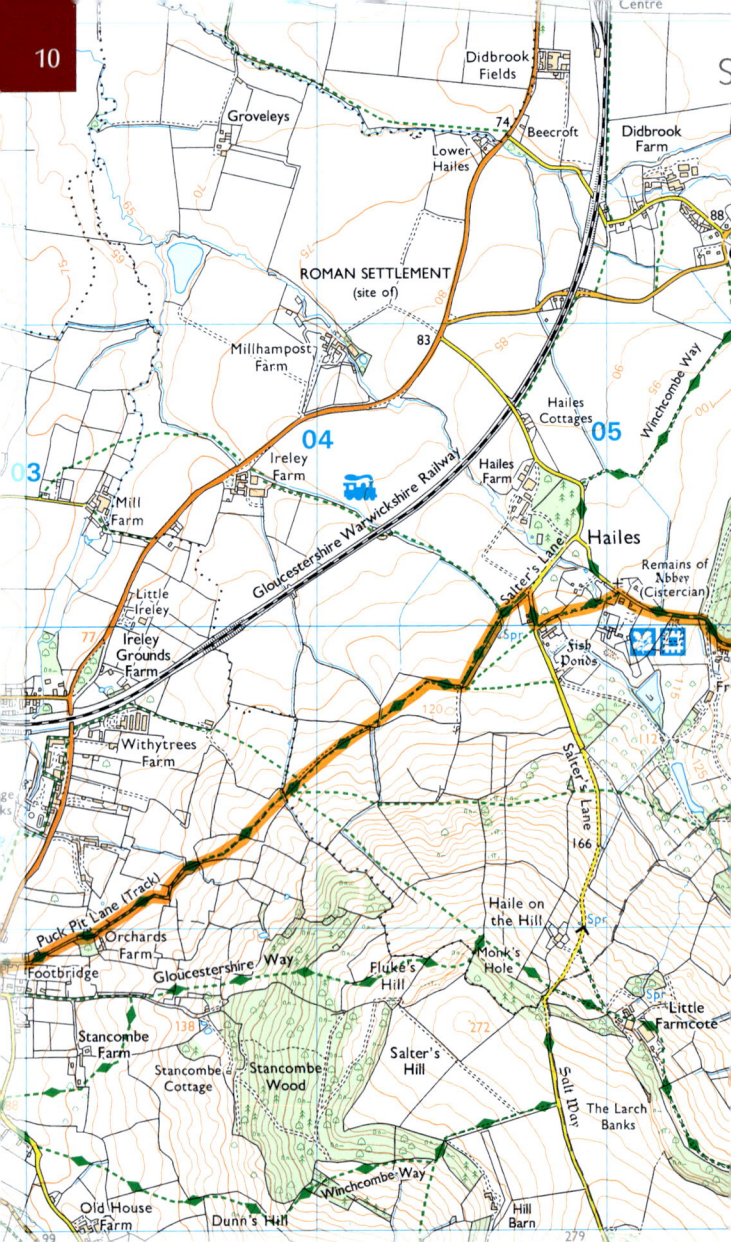

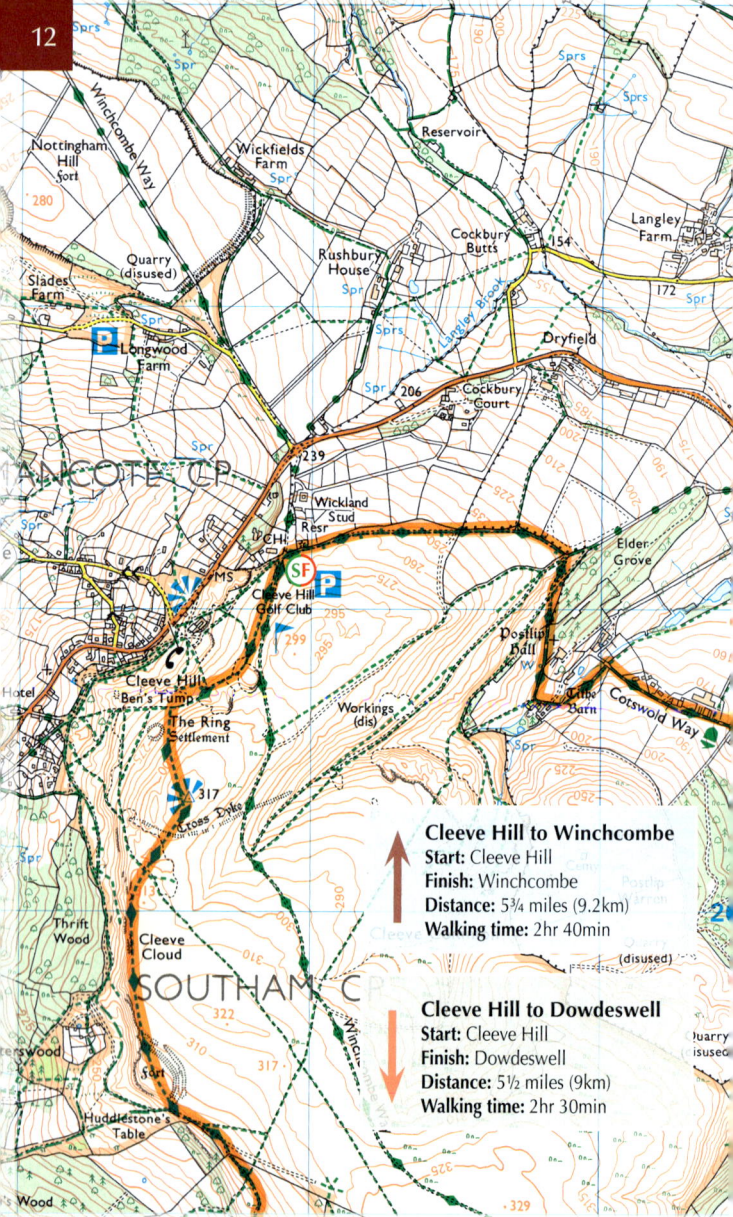

Cleeve Hill to Winchcombe
Start: Cleeve Hill
Finish: Winchcombe
Distance: 5¾ miles (9.2km)
Walking time: 2hr 40min

Cleeve Hill to Dowdeswell
Start: Cleeve Hill
Finish: Dowdeswell
Distance: 5½ miles (9km)
Walking time: 2hr 30min

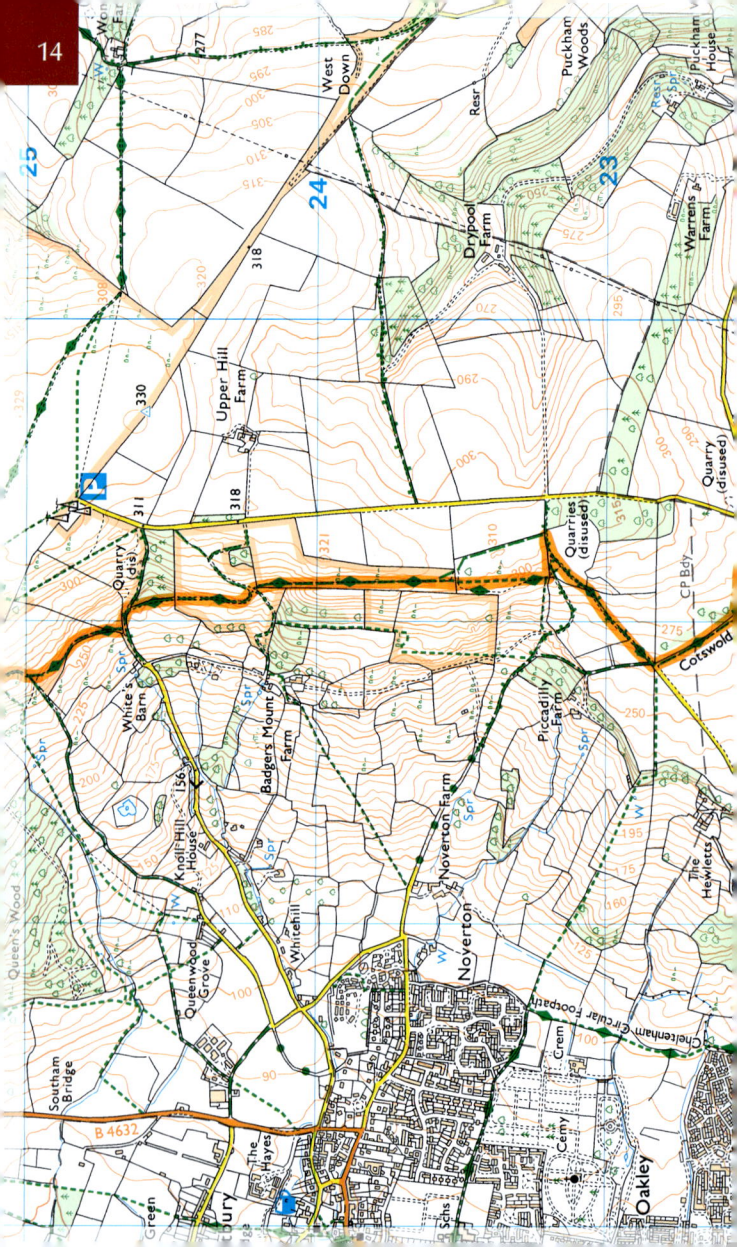

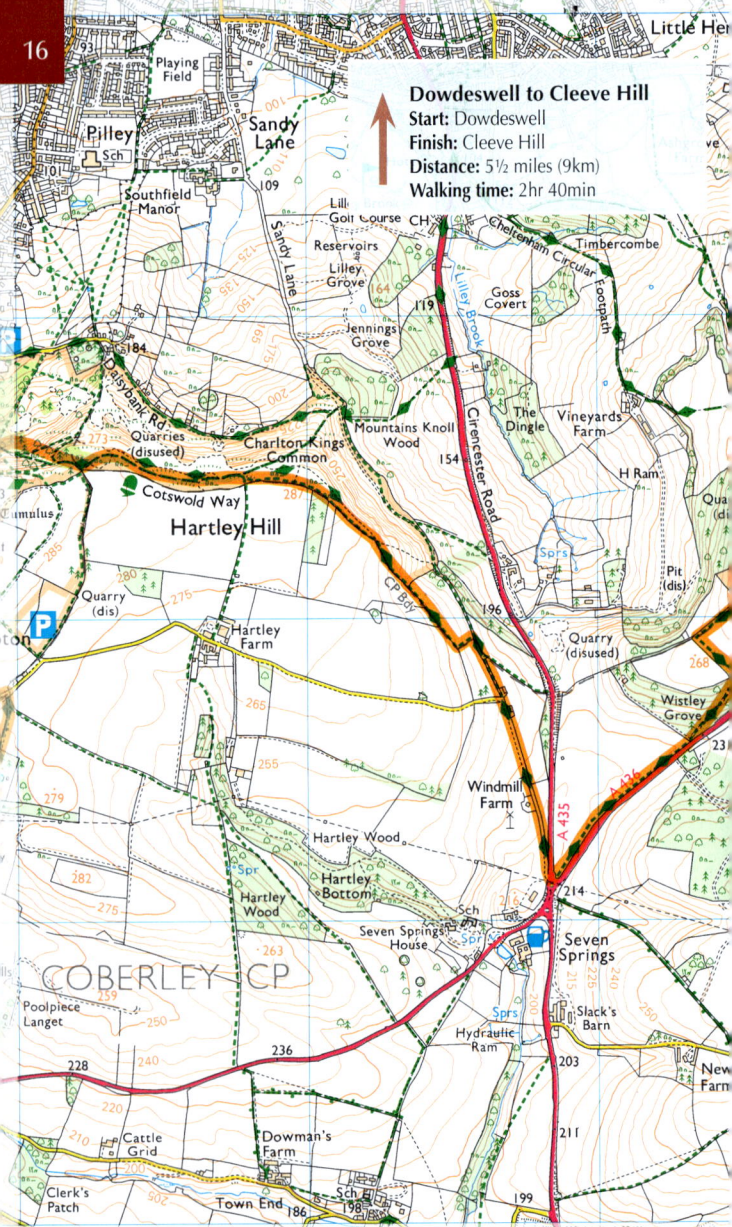

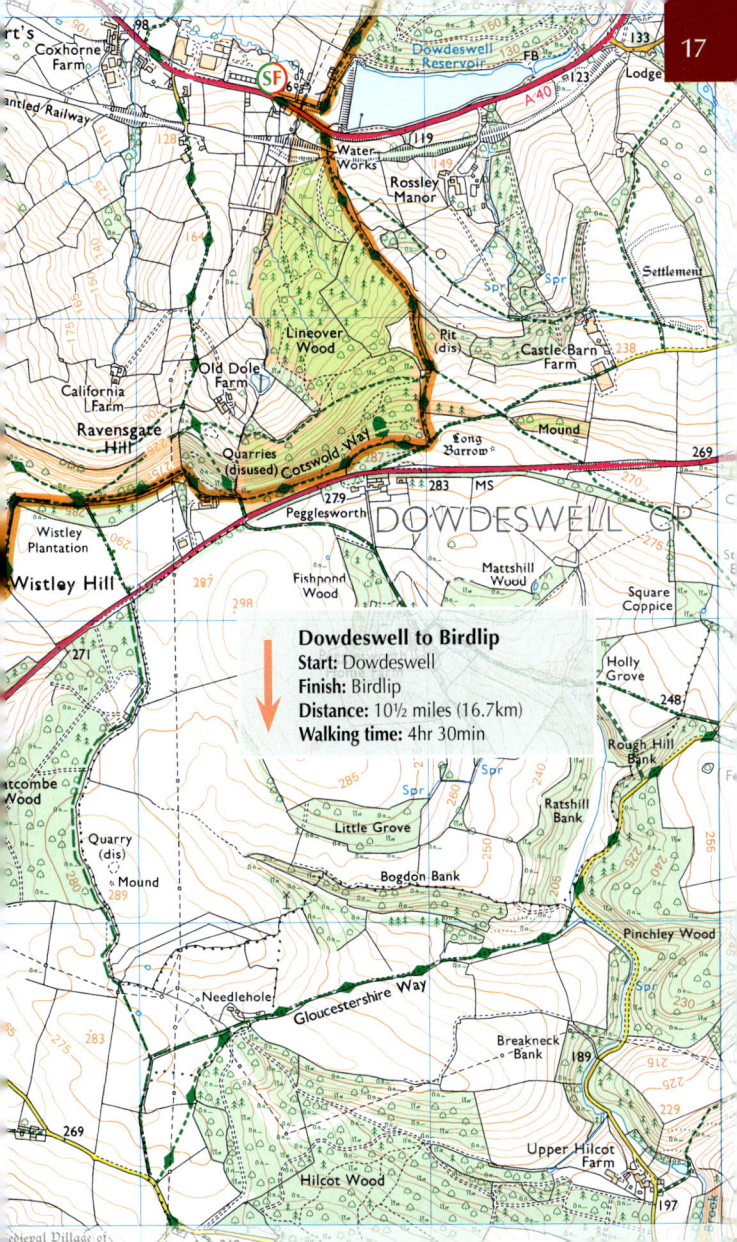

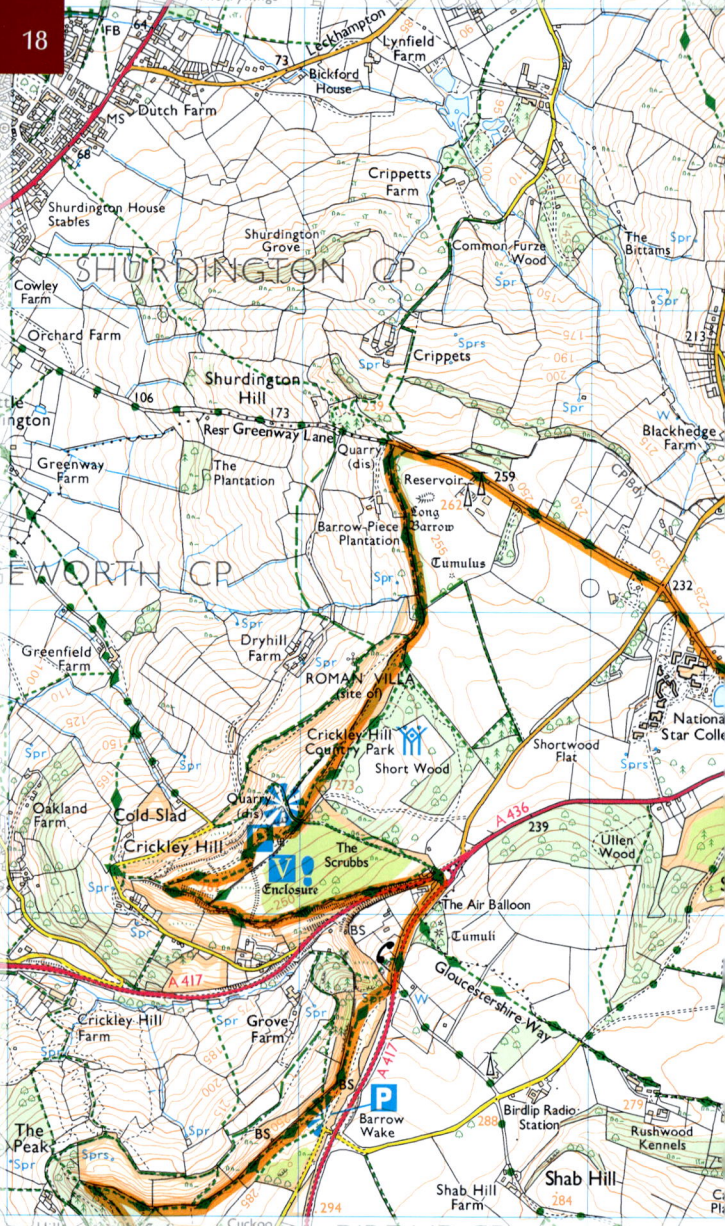

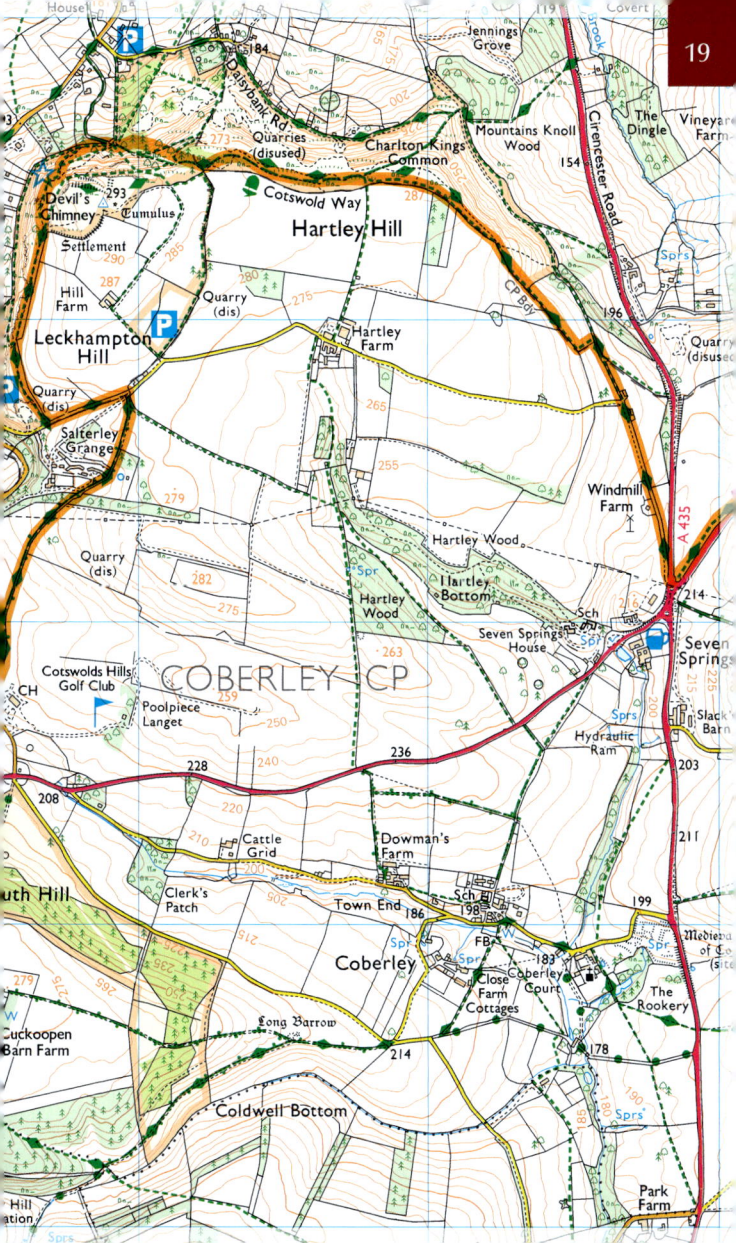

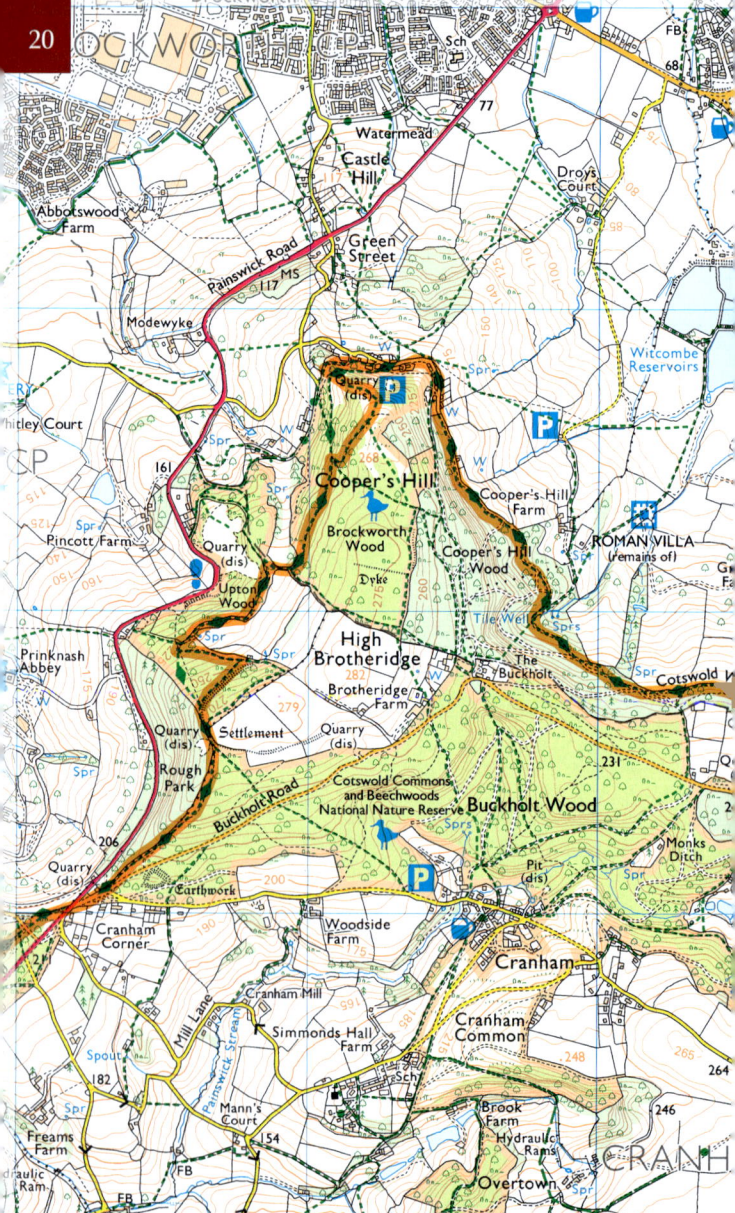

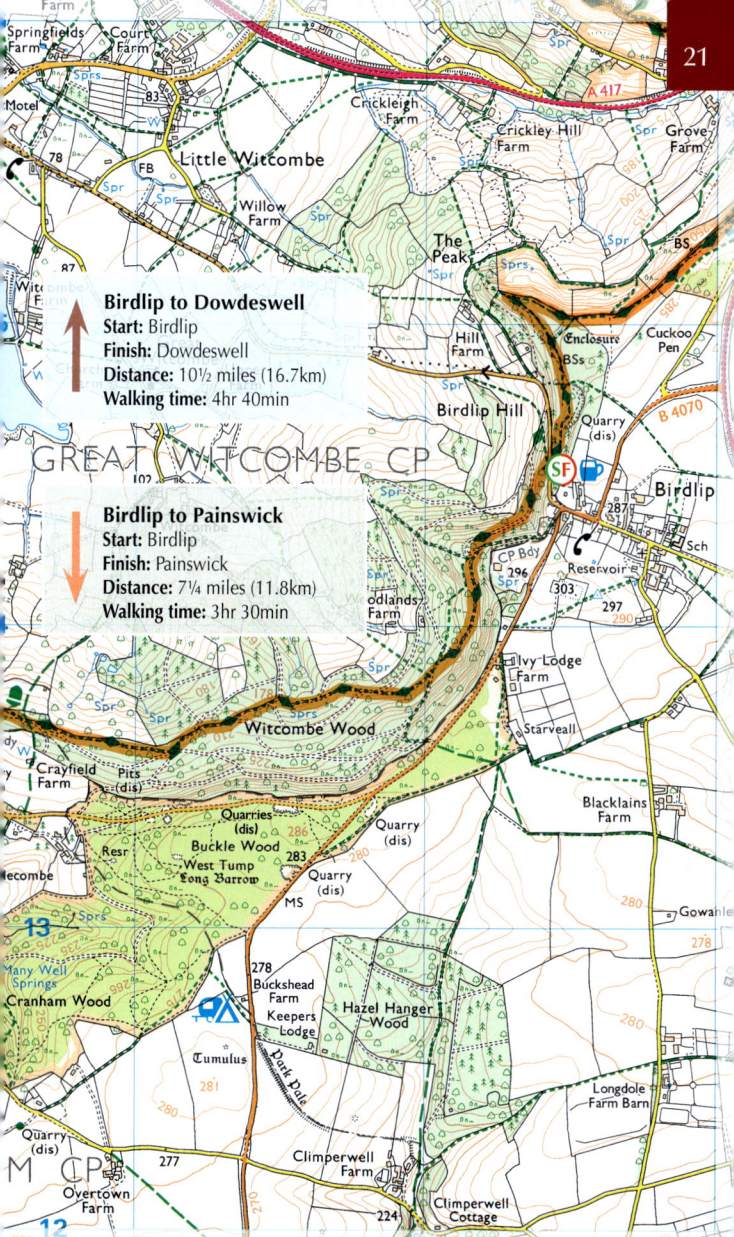

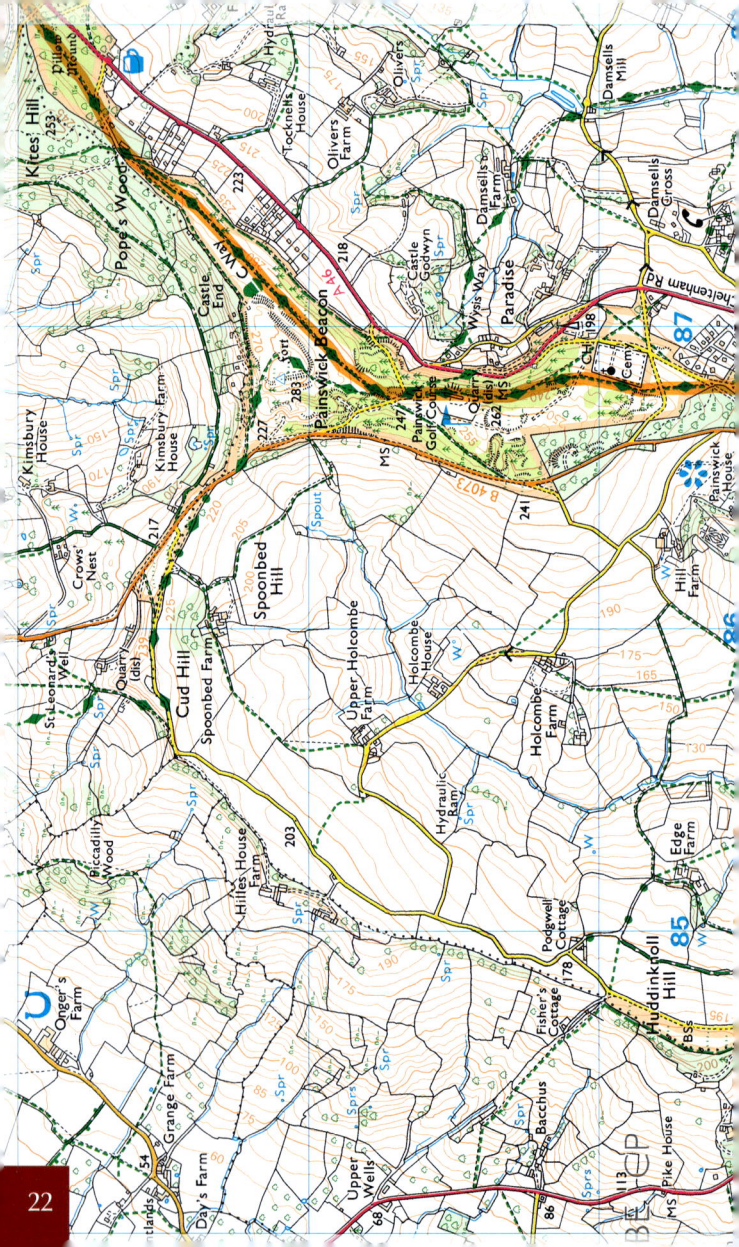

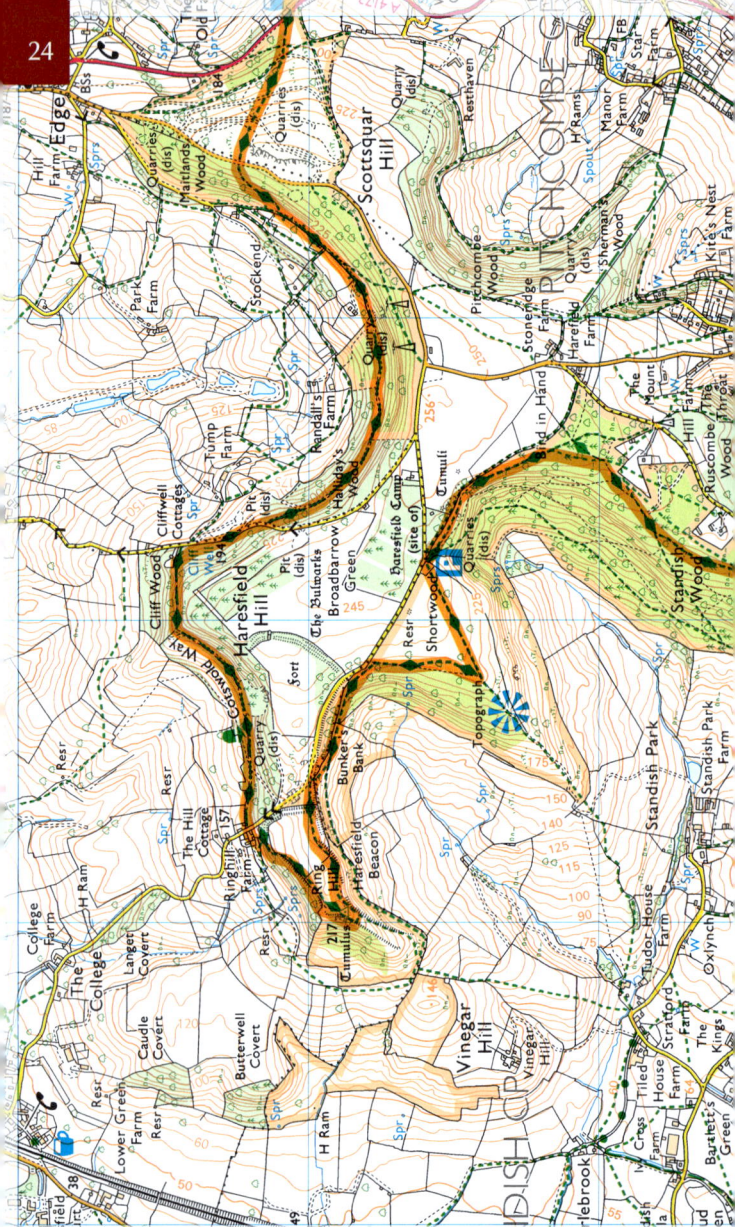

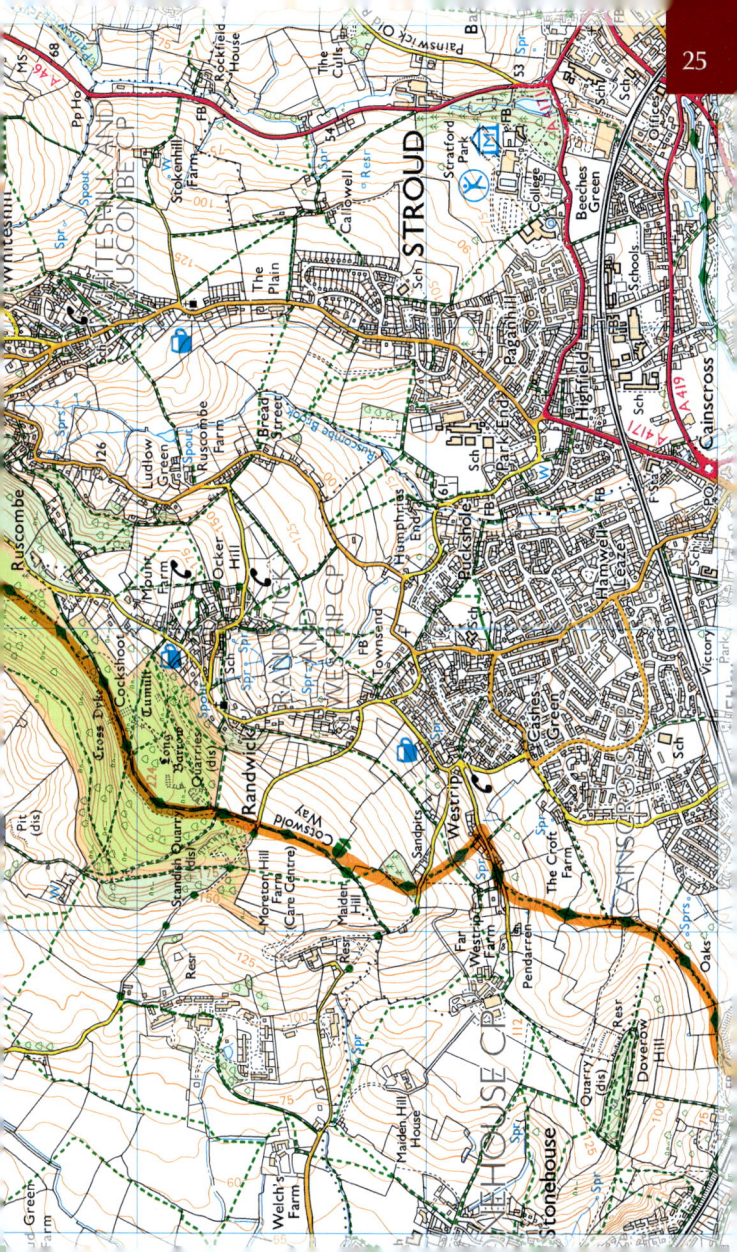

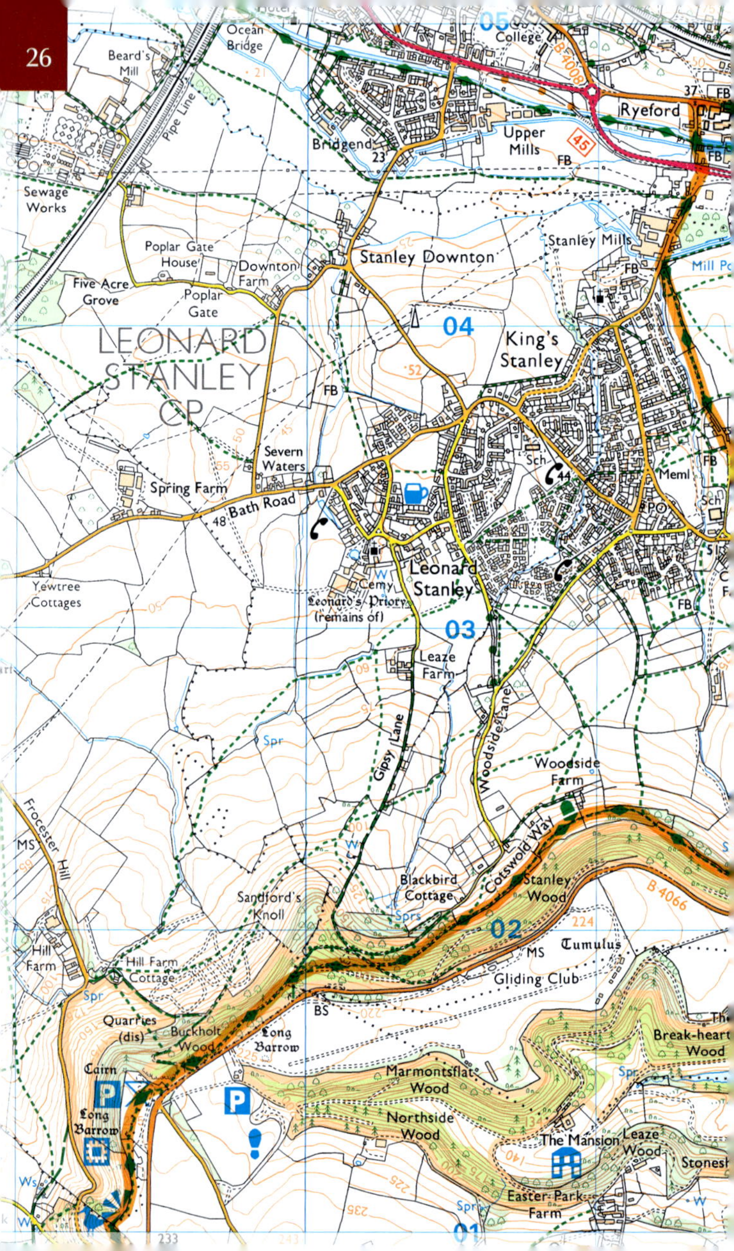

Ocean Bridge
Beard's Mill
College
B 4008
Ryeford
Bridgend
Upper Mills
Sewage Works
Pipe Line
Poplar Gate House
Downton Farm
Stanley Downton
Stanley Mills
Mill Pond
Five Acre Grove
Poplar Gate
LEONARD STANLEY CP
King's Stanley
FB
Sch
Meml
PO
Severn Waters
Spring Farm
Bath Road
Leonard Stanley
Cemy
Leonard's Priory (remains of)
Yewtree Cottages
Leaze Farm
Spr
Gipsy Lane
Woodside Lane
Woodside Farm
Frocester Hill
MS
Cotswold Way
Blackbird Cottage
Stanley Wood
B 4066
Sandford's Knoll
Sprs
Tumulus
Hill Farm
Hill Farm Cottage
Gliding Club
BS
Quarries (dis)
Buckholt Wood
Long Barrow
The Break-heart Wood
Cairn
Marmontsflat Wood
Long Barrow
Northside Wood
The Mansion
Leaze Wood
Easter Park Farm
Stonehouse
Ws

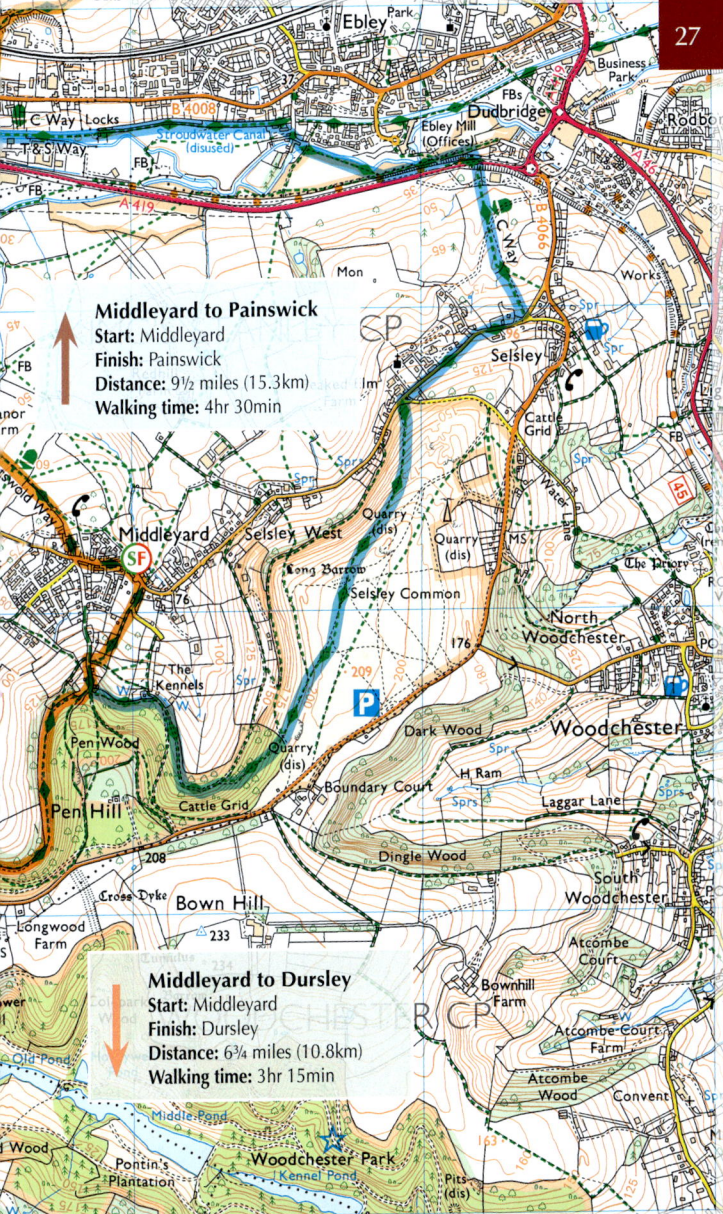

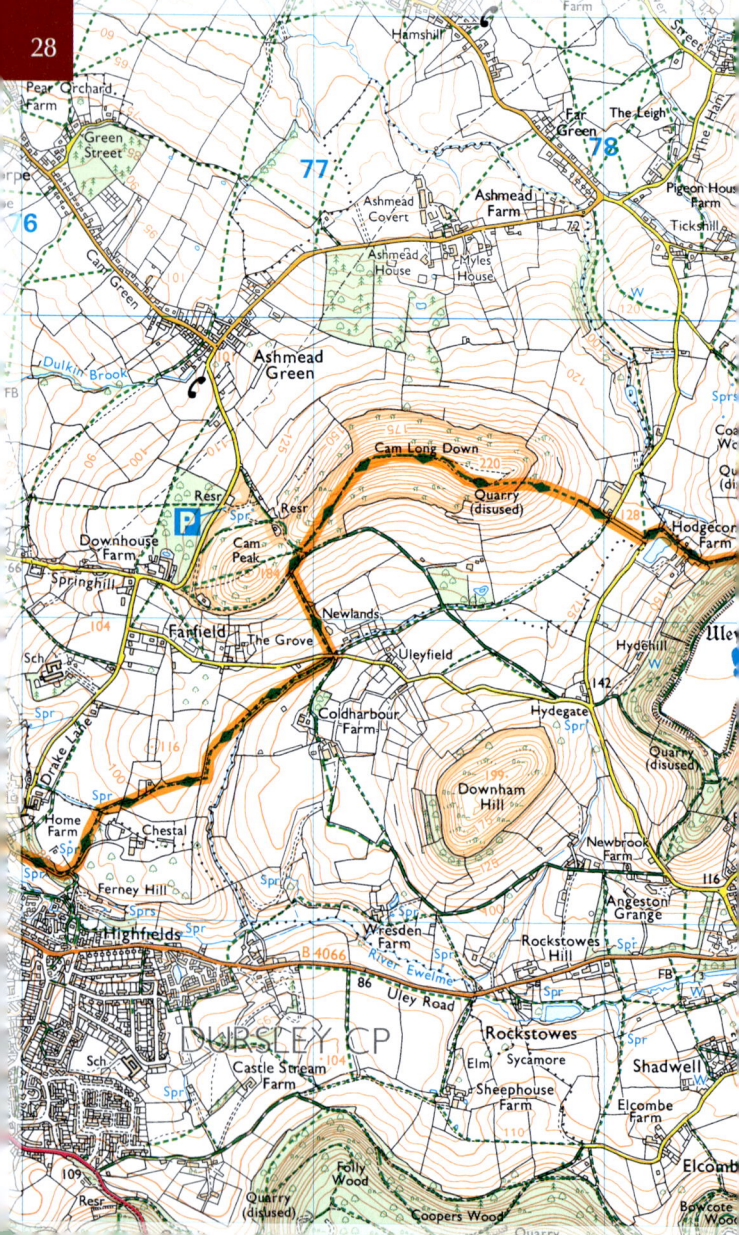

Dursley to Middleyard
Start: Dursley
Finish: Middleyard
Distance: 6¾ miles (10.8km)
Walking time: 3hr 30min

Dursley to Wotton-under-Edge
Start: Dursley
Finish: Wotton-under-Edge
Distance: 7¾ miles (12.5km)
Walking time: 3hr 30min

Wotton-under-Edge to Dursley
Start: Wotton-under-Edge
Finish: Dursley
Distance: 7¾ miles (12.5km)
Walking time: 3hr 30min

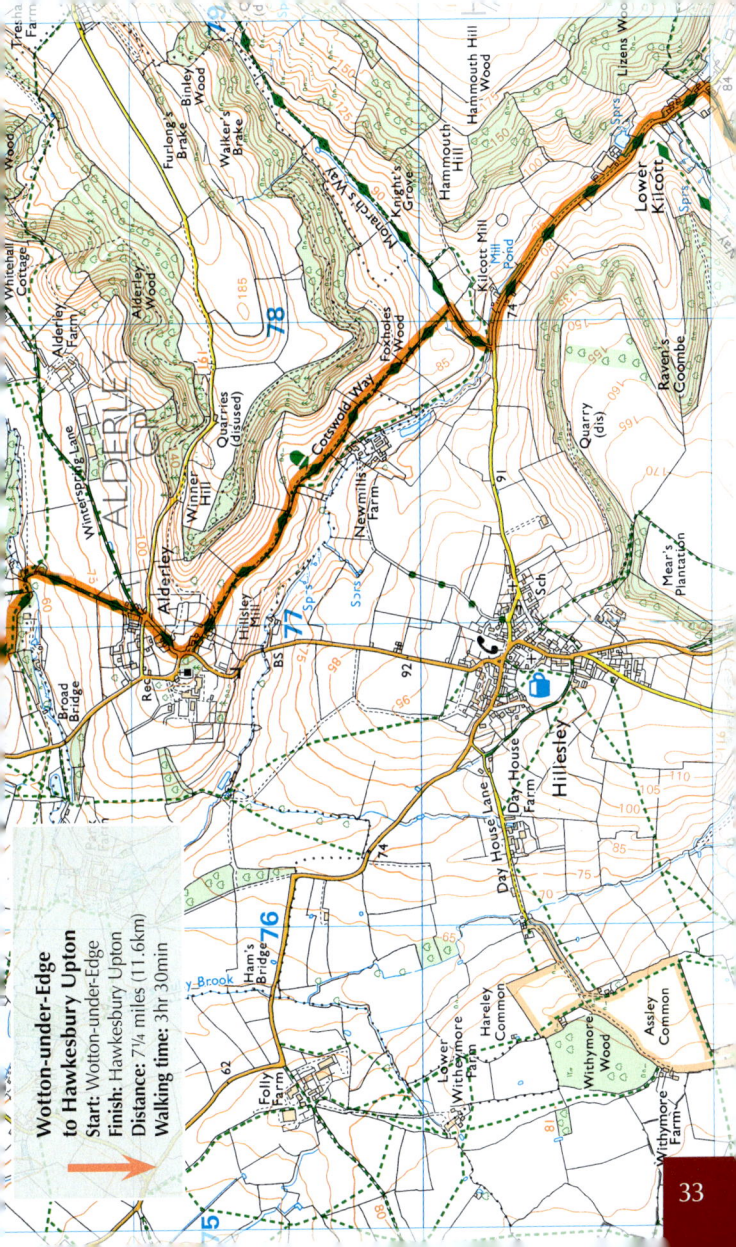

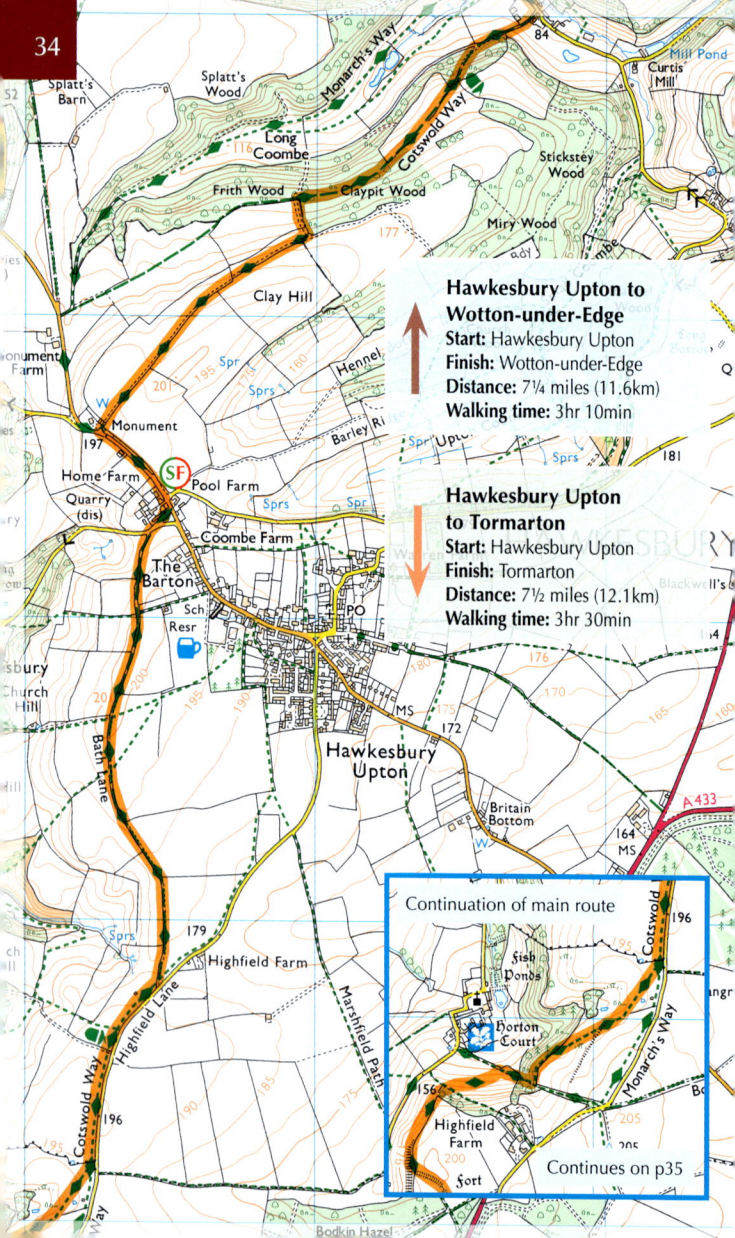

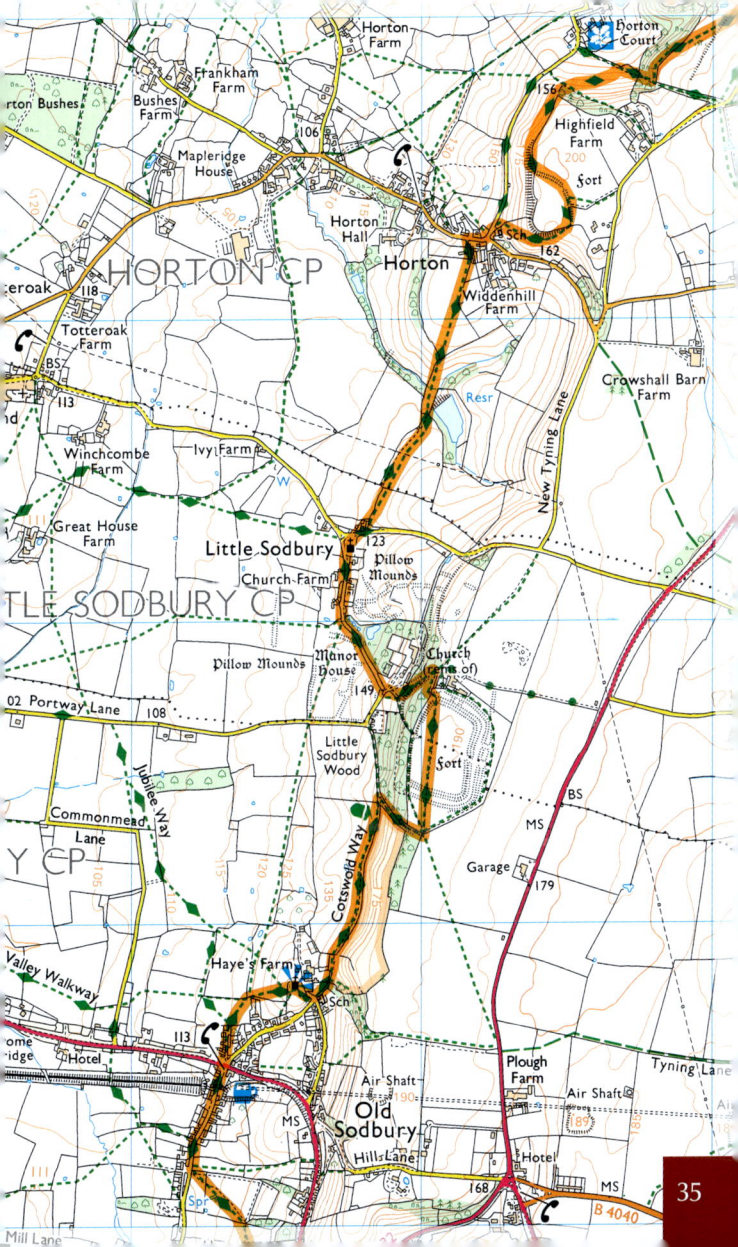

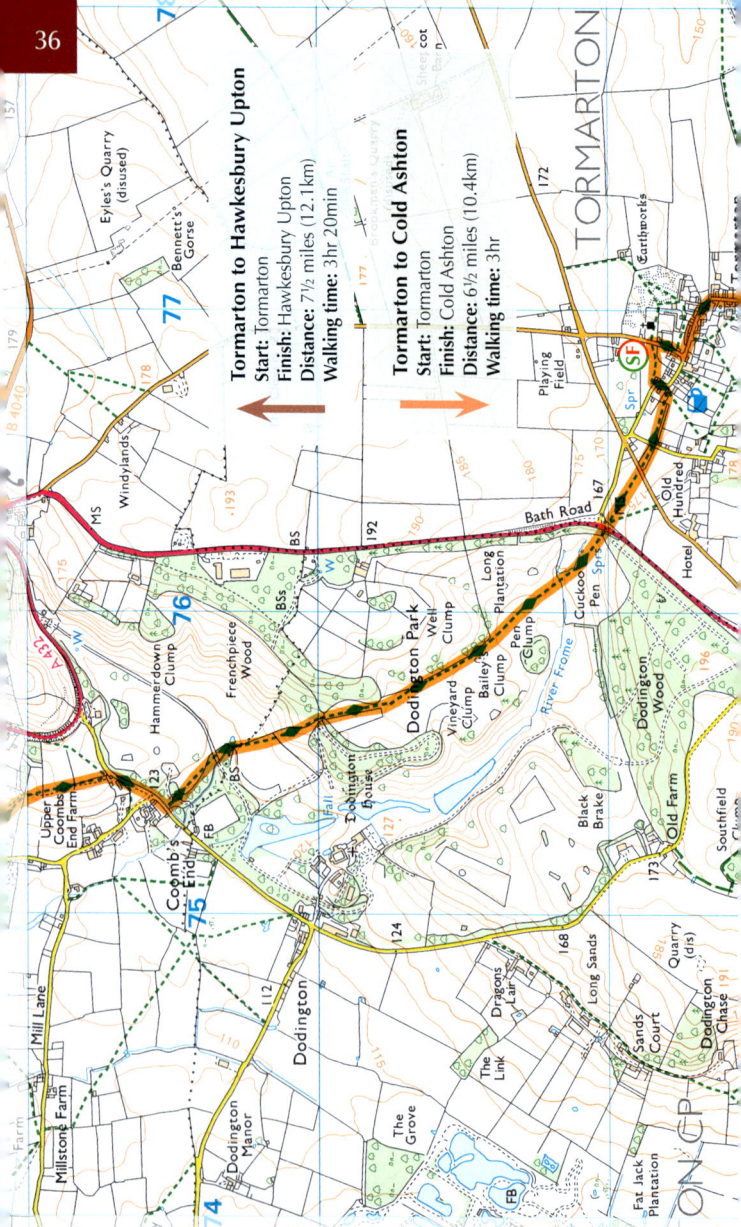

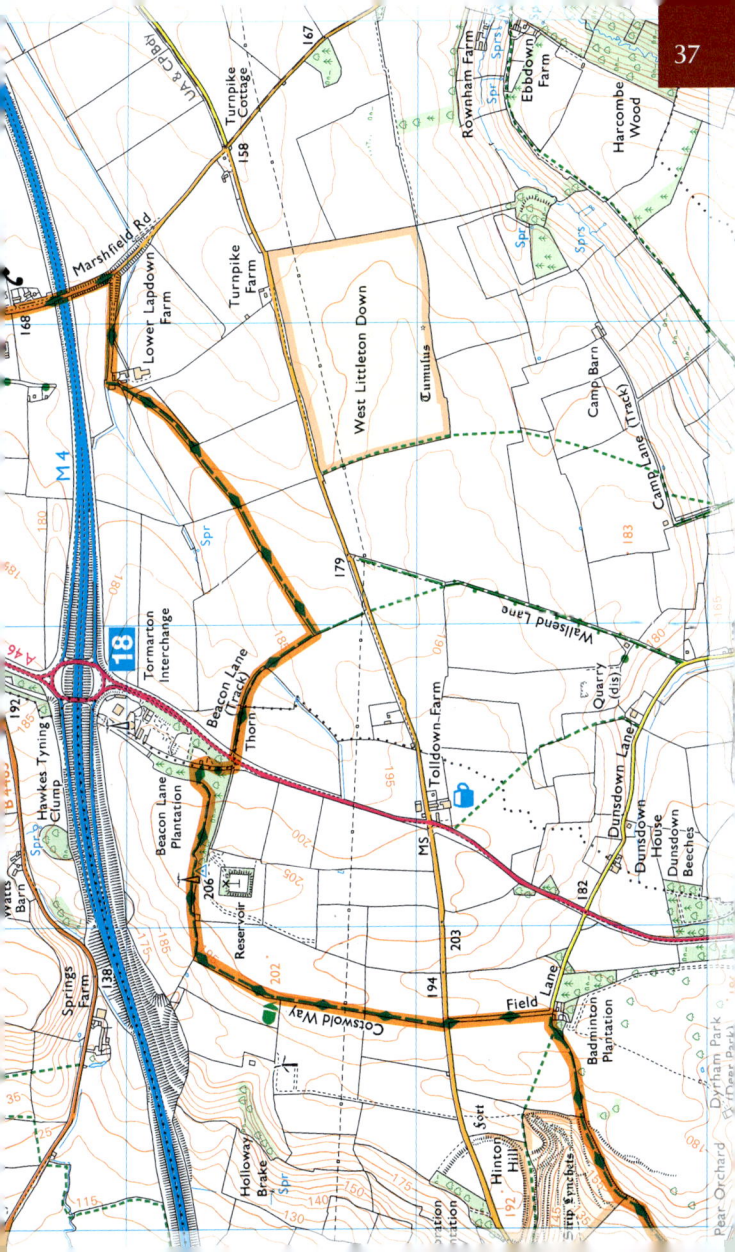

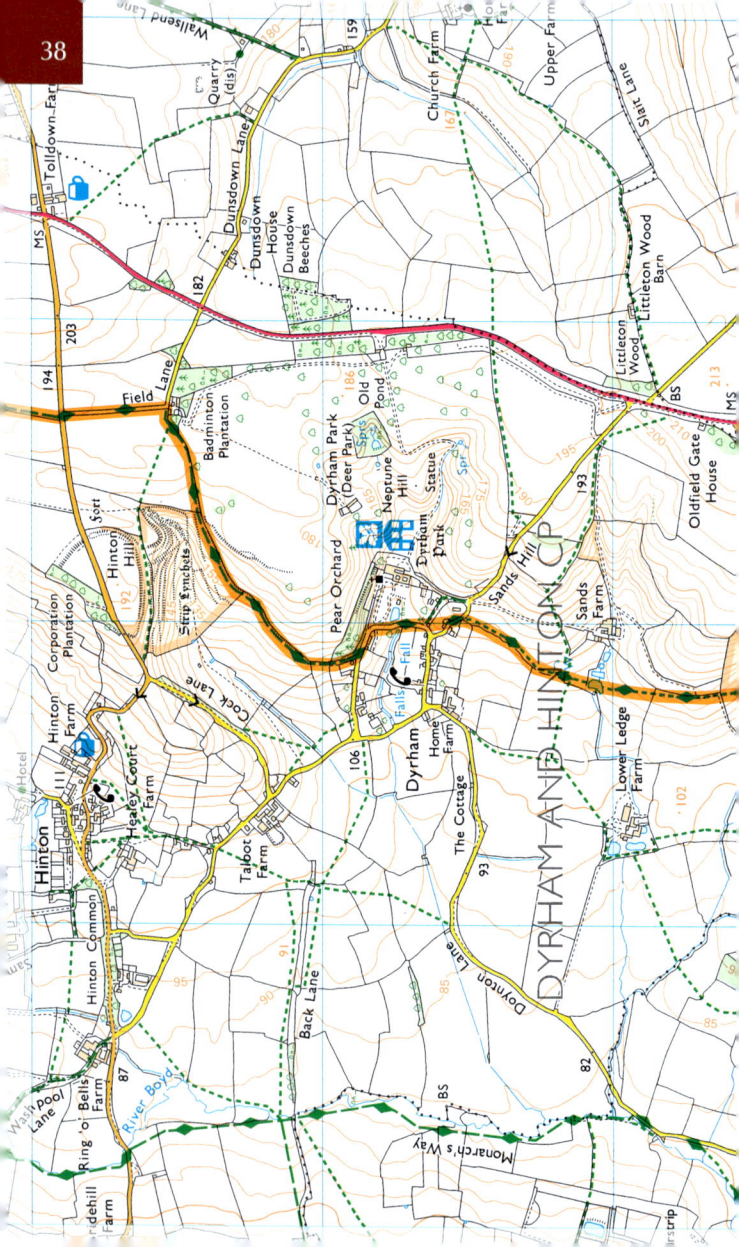

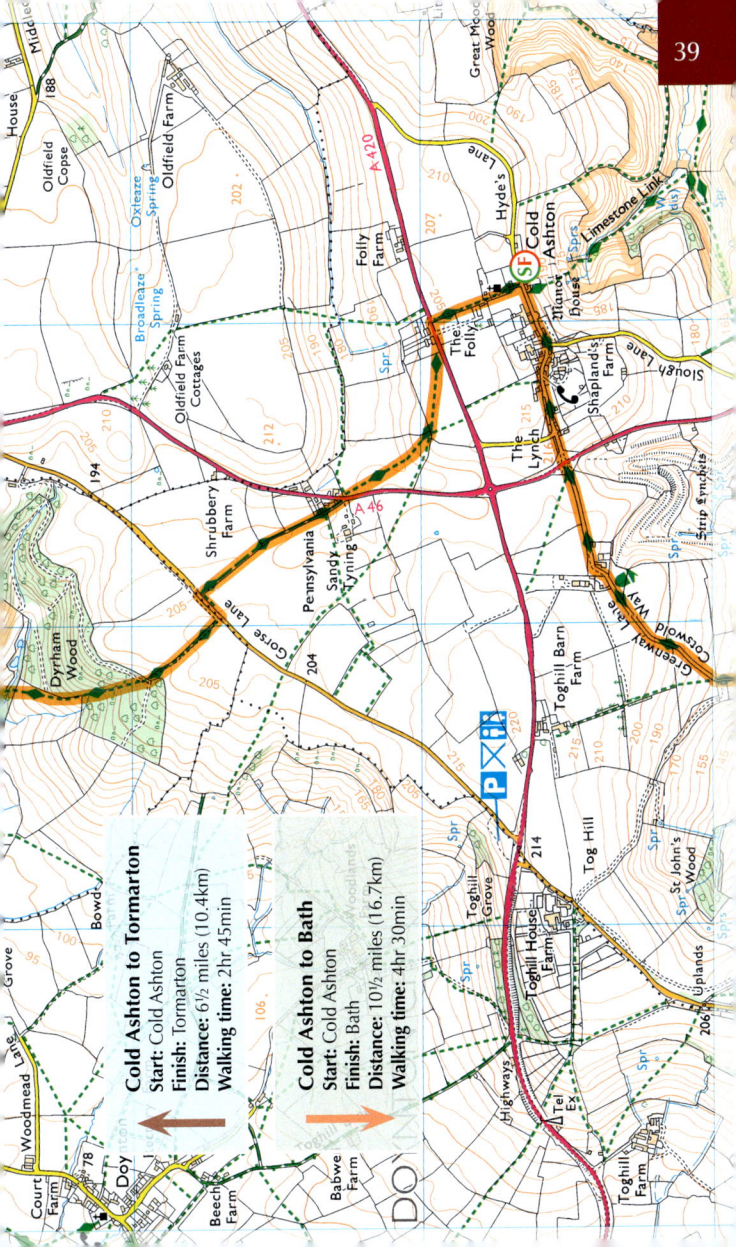

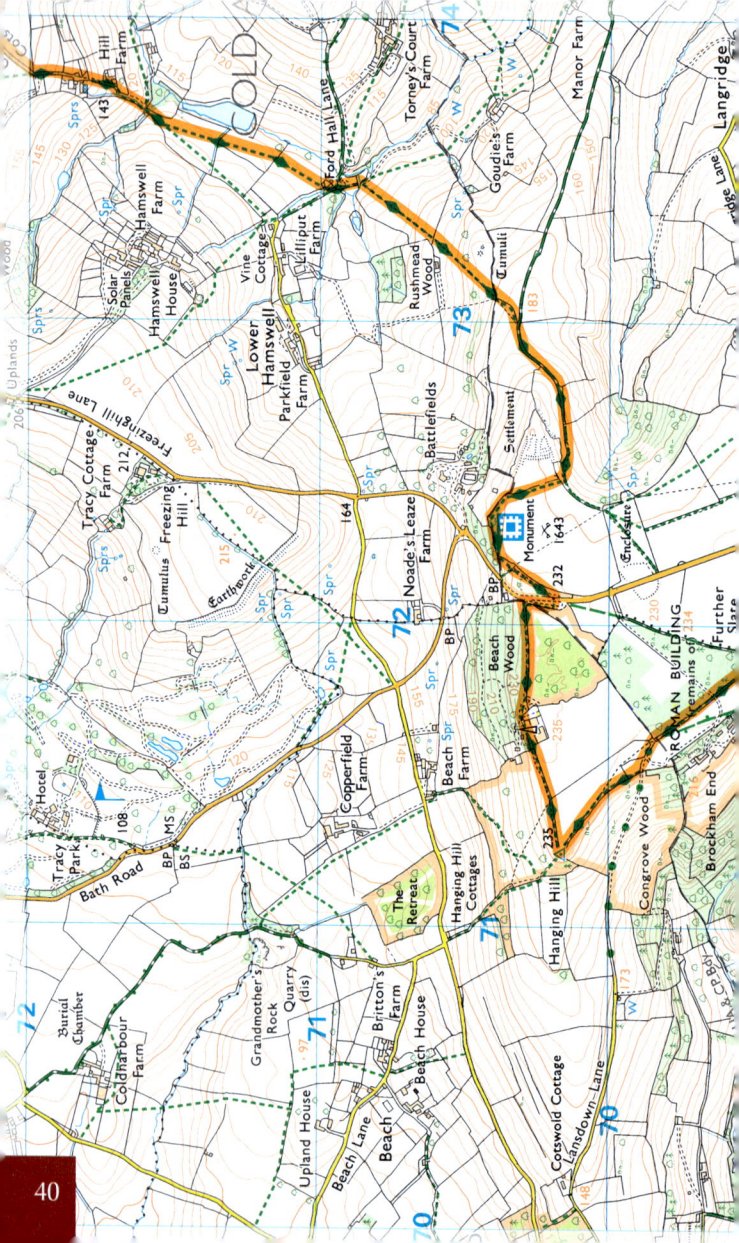

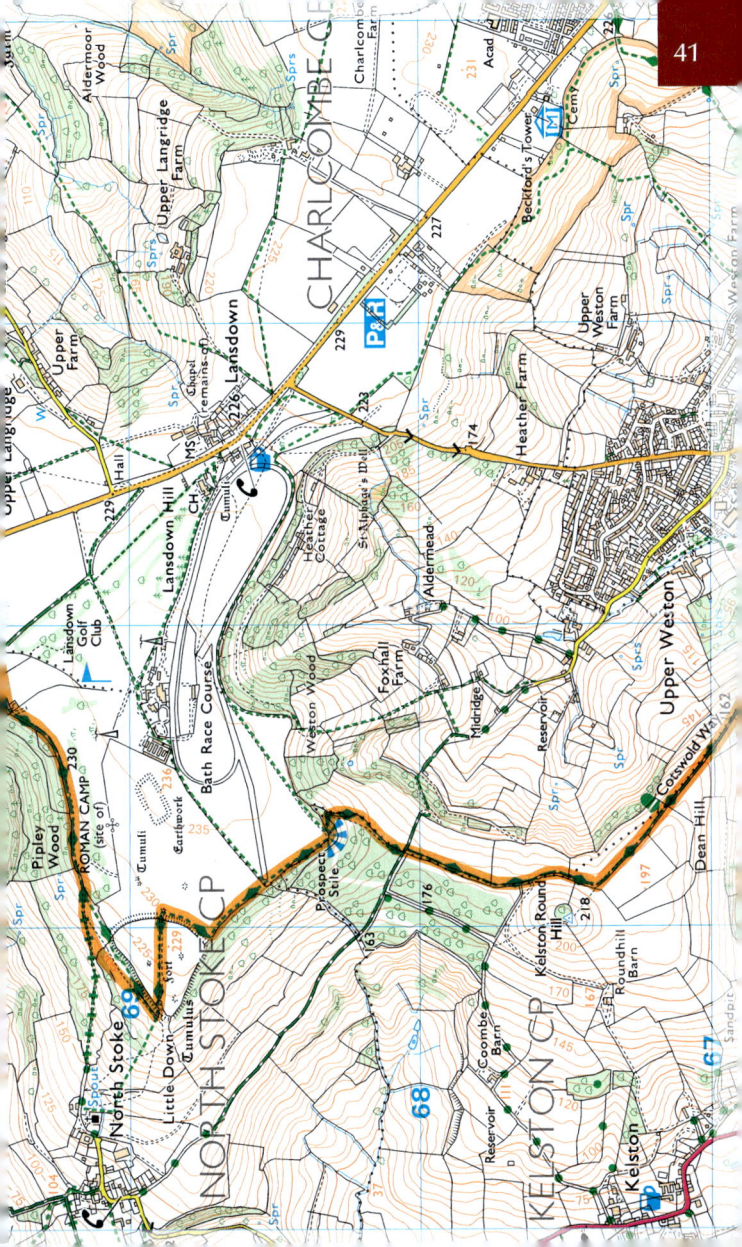

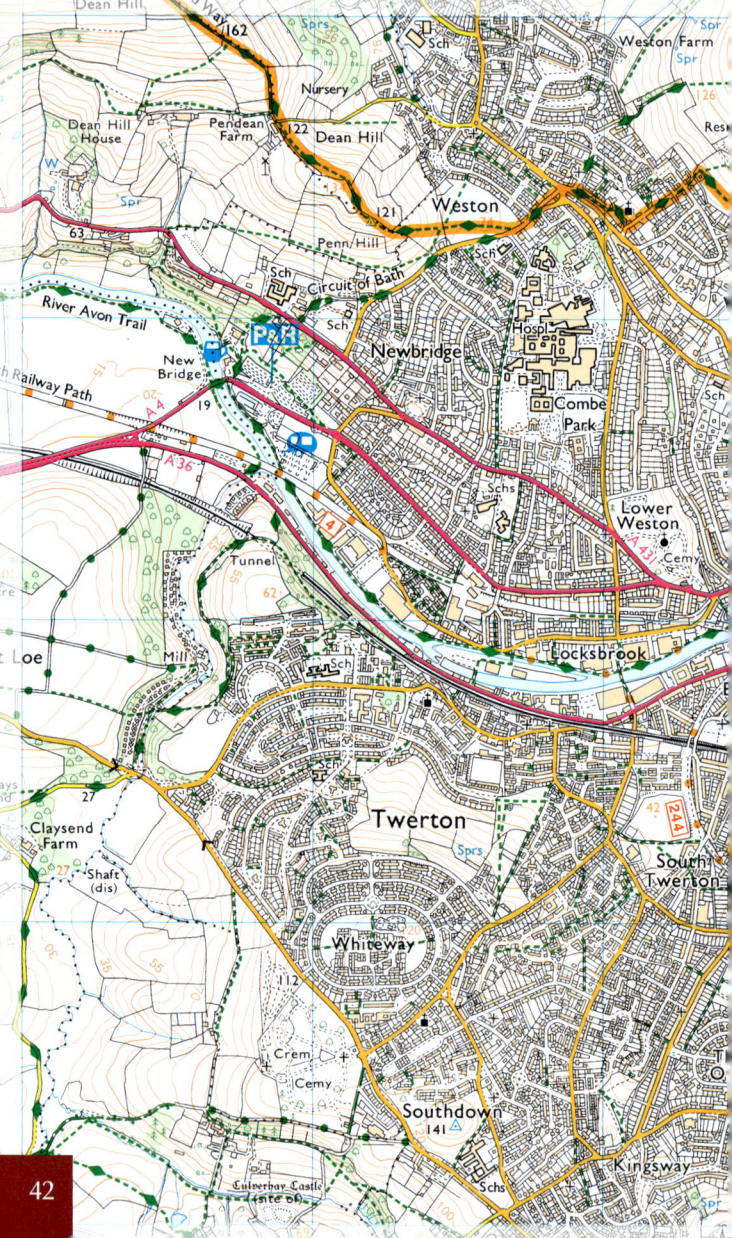

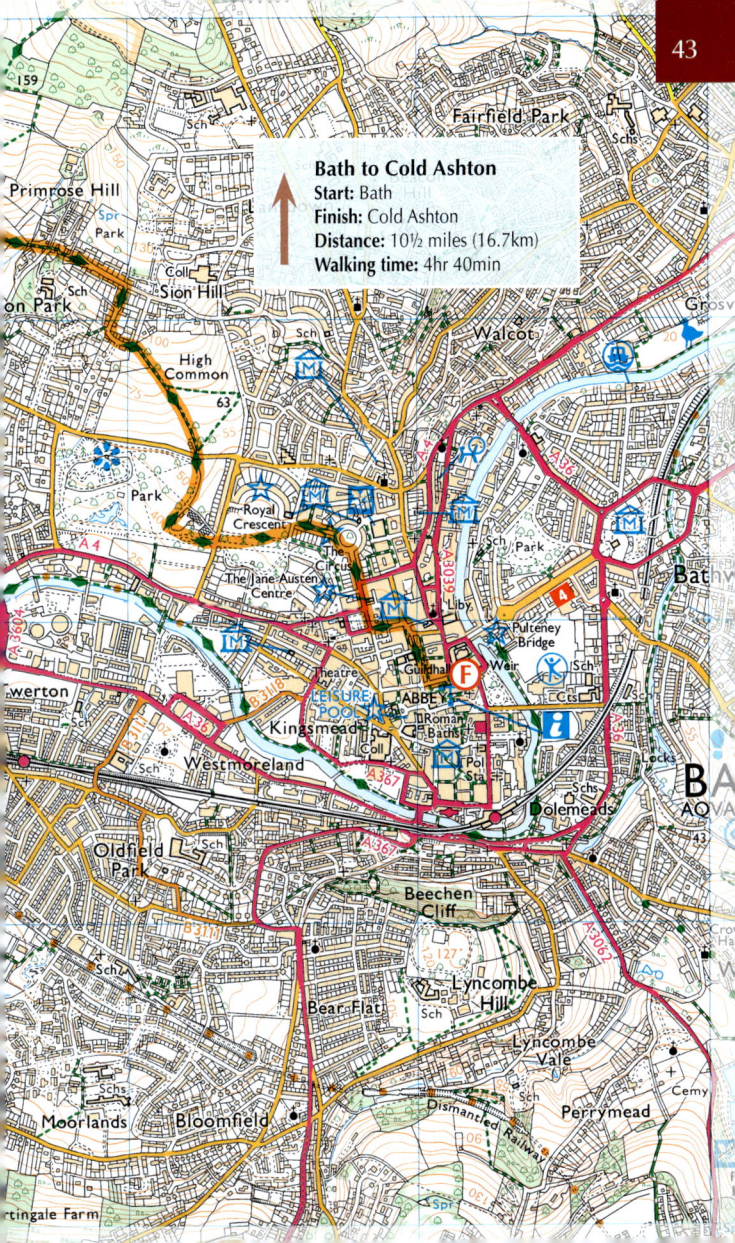

LEGEND OF SYMBOLS USED ON ORDNANCE SURVEY 1:25,000 (EXPLORER®) MAPPING

ROADS AND PATHS — Not necessarily rights of way

M1 or A6(M)	Motorway
A 35	Dual carriageway
A30	Main road
B 3074	Secondary road
	Narrow road with passing places
	Road under construction
	Road generally more than 4 m wide
	Road generally less than 4 m wide
	Other road, drive or track, fenced and unfenced
	Gradient: steeper than 20% (1 in 5); 14% (1 in 7) to 20% (1 in 5)
Ferry	Ferry; Ferry P – passenger only
	Path

- Ⓢ Service Area
- Ⓢ Service Area
- 7 Junction Number
- T1 Toll road junction

RAILWAYS

- Multiple track / Single track — standard gauge
- Narrow gauge or Light rapid transit system (LRTS) and station
- Road over; road under; level crossing
- Cutting; tunnel; embankment
- Station, open to passengers; siding

PUBLIC RIGHTS OF WAY

- ---------- Footpath
- — — — Bridleway
- +++++ Byway open to all traffic
- – – – – Restricted byway

The representation on this map of any other road, track or path is no evidence of the existence of a right of way

ARCHAEOLOGICAL AND HISTORICAL INFORMATION

Symbol	Description	Symbol	Description	Symbol	Description
✢	Site of antiquity	VILLA	Roman	☆	Visible earthwork
⚔ 1066	Site of battle (with date)	𝕮𝖆𝖘𝖙𝖑𝖊	Non-Roman		

Information provided by English Heritage for England and the Royal Commissions on the Ancient and Historical Monuments for Scotland and Wales

OTHER PUBLIC ACCESS

• • • Other routes with public access — The exact nature of the rights on these routes and the existence of any restrictions may be checked with the local highway authority. Alignments are based on the best information available

♦ ♦ ♦ Recreational route

♦ ♦ ♦ **National Trail**   (♦) Long Distance Route

- - - - Permissive footpath ⎫ Footpaths and bridleways along which landowners have permitted public use but which are not rights of way. The agreement may be withdrawn
— — — Permissive bridleway ⎭

• • • Traffic-free cycle route

[1] **1** National cycle network route number – traffic free; on road

ACCESS LAND

 Firing and test ranges in the area. Danger! Observe warning notices

 Access permitted within managed controls, for example, local byelaws. Visit www.access.mod.uk for information

England and Wales

 Access land boundary and tint

 Access land in wooded area

i Access information point

Portrayal of access land on this map is intended as a guide to land which is normally available for access on foot, for example access land created under the Countryside and Rights of Way Act 2000, and land managed by the National Trust, Forestry Commission and Woodland Trust. Access for other activities may also exist. Some restrictions will apply; some land will be excluded from open access rights. The depiction of rights of access does not imply or express any warranty as to its accuracy or completeness. Observe local signs and follow the Countryside Code.
Visit www.countrysideaccess.gov.uk for up-to-date information

BOUNDARIES

— + — + — National

— · — · — County (England)

— — — — Unitary Authority (UA), Metropolitan District (Met Dist), London Borough (LB) or District (Scotland & Wales are solely Unitary Authorities)

· · · · · · · · Civil Parish (CP) (England) or Community (C) (Wales)

▬▬▬ National Park boundary

VEGETATION

Limits of vegetation are defined by positioning of symbols

♣ ♣   Coniferous trees

○ ○   Non-coniferous trees

⁰⁰ ⁰⁰   Coppice

○ ○ ○   Orchard

⁞ ⁞   Scrub

ıı. ıı.   Bracken, heath or rough grassland

   Marsh, reeds or saltings

HEIGHTS AND NATURAL FEATURES

52 ·	Ground survey height
284 ·	Air survey height

Surface heights are to the nearest metre above mean sea level. Where two heights are shown, the first height is to the base of the triangulation pillar and the second (in brackets) to the highest natural point of the hill

Vertical face/cliff

Loose rock · Boulders · Outcrop · Scree

Contours are at 5 or 10 metre vertical intervals

- Water
- Mud
- Sand; sand and shingle

SELECTED TOURIST AND LEISURE INFORMATION

- Building of historic interest
- Cadw
- Heritage centre
- Camp site
- Caravan site
- Camping and caravan site
- Castle / fort
- Cathedral / Abbey
- Craft centre
- Country park
- Cycle trail
- Mountain bike trail
- Cycle hire
- English Heritage
- Fishing
- Forestry Commission Visitor centre
- Garden / arboretum
- Golf course or links
- Historic Scotland
- Information centre, all year
- Information centre, seasonal
- Horse riding
- Museum
- National Park Visitor Centre (park logo) e.g. Yorkshire Dales
- Nature reserve
- National Trust
- Other tourist feature
- Parking
- Park and ride, all year
- Park and ride, seasonal
- Picnic site
- Preserved railway
- Public Convenience
- Public house/s
- Recreation / leisure / sports centre
- Roman site (Hadrian's Wall only)
- Slipway
- Telephone, emergency
- Telephone, public
- Telephone, roadside assistance
- Theme / pleasure park
- Viewpoint
- Visitor centre
- Walks / trails
- World Heritage site / area
- Water activites
- Boat trips
- Boat hire

(For complete legend and symbols, see any OS Explorer® map).

Broadway Tower (Stage 1)

The Cotswold Way

This map booklet accompanies the latest edition of Cicerone's guidebook to walking The Cotswold Way National Trail, described in full in both directions. The guidebook features annotated 1:100,000 mapping alongside detailed step-by-step route desription and full planning information.

OTHER CICERONE TRAIL GUIDES

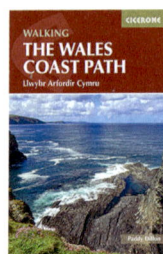
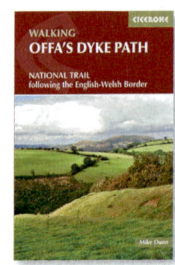

Cicerone National Trails Guides
The South West Coast Path
The South Downs Way
The North Downs Way
The Ridgeway National Trail
The Thames Path
The Cotswold Way
The Peddars Way and
  Norfolk Coast Path
The Cleveland Way and
  the Yorkshire Wolds Way
Cycling the Pennine Bridleway
The Pennine Way
Hadrian's Wall Path
The Pembrokeshire Coast Path
Offa's Dyke Path
Glyndŵr's Way
The Southern Upland Way
The Speyside Way
The West Highland Way
The Great Glen Way

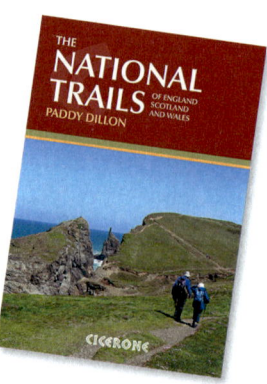

Visit our website for a full
list of Cicerone Trail Guides
www.cicerone.co.uk